CHUNGKINGOSAURUS
and Other Plated Dinosaurs
by Dougal Dixon

illustrated by
Steve Weston and James Field

PICTURE WINDOW BOOKS
Minneapolis, Minnesota

Picture Window Books
5115 Excelsior Boulevard
Suite 232
Minneapolis, MN 55416
877-845-8392
www.picturewindowbooks.com

 All books published by Picture Window Books
are manufactured with paper containing at
least 10 percent post-consumer waste.

Library of Congress Cataloging-in-Publication Data
Dixon, Dougal.
Chungkingosaurus and other plated dinosaurs / by
Dougal Dixon ; illustrated by Steve Weston &
James Field.
p. cm. — (Dinosaur find)
Includes index.
ISBN-13: 978-1-4048-4014-0 (library binding)
1. Chungkingosaurus—Juvenile literature.
2. Ornithischia—Juvenile literature. I. Weston, Steve,
ill. II. Field, James, ill. III. Title.
QE862.O65D5855 2008
567.915—dc22   2007040923

Acknowledgments
This book was produced for Picture Window Books
by Bender Richardson White, U.K.

Illustrations by James Field (cover and pages 4–5,
7, 11, 15, 19) and Steve Weston (9, 13, 17, 21).
Diagrams by Stefan Chabluk.

Photographs: istockphotos pages 10 (Joe Gough),
12 (Giacomo Nodari), 16 (Paul Cowan), 18, 20
(Ian Scott); bigstock photos 6 (Marion Wear), 8
(Girolamo Langella); Frank Lane Photo Library
(Chris Mattison).

Consultant: John Stidworthy, Scientific Fellow of
the Zoological Society, London, and former
Lecturer in the Education Department, Natural
History Museum, London.

Types of dinosaurs
In this book, a red shape at the
top of a left-hand page shows
the animal was a meat-eater.
A green shape shows it was
a plant-eater.

Just how big—or small—
were they?
Dinosaurs were many different
sizes. We have compared their
size to one of the following:

 Chicken
2 feet (60 centimeters) tall
Weight 6 pounds (2.7 kilograms)

 Adult person
6 feet (1.8 meters) tall
Weight 170 pounds (76.5 kg)

 Elephant
10 feet (3 m) tall
Weight 12,000 pounds
(5,400 kg)

TABLE OF CONTENTS

WHAT'S INSIDE?

Plated dinosaurs! These animals lived
in many places in the prehistoric
world. Find out how they survived
millions of years ago and what they
have in common with today's animals.

PLATED DINOSAURS

Dinosaurs lived between 230 million and 65 million years ago. There were many different kinds of dinosaurs. One kind was the plated dinosaur. These dinosaurs had bones that grew into flat plates or scutes. Other bones became spikes or spines. The bones grew on their backs, tails, and sides. Plates and spikes were used for protection, for show, and to control body heat.

Halfway through the age of dinosaurs, plated dinosaurs roamed the plains of what is now North America. There, *Stegosaurus* shared its ground with *Hesperosaurus*.

HUAYANGOSAURUS

Pronunciation:
hwi-YANG-uh-SAW-rus

Huayangosaurus was one of the world's first plated dinosaurs. It had two rows of narrow plates on its back. Spikes grew on its shoulders and tail. It lived in forests with long-necked dinosaurs.

Spiky animals today

Like *Huayangosaurus* once was, the modern spider crab is covered in spikes and narrow plates to help keep it safe.

Size Comparison

Huayangosaurus had spikes on its shoulders and tail, as well as plates on its neck and back.

LEXOVISAURUS

Pronunciation:
lek-SOH-vi-SAW-rus

The life of a plated dinosaur was difficult. *Lexovisaurus* had to fight off attacks from meat-eaters such as *Megalosaurus*. It used back plates and tail spikes to defend itself. The dinosaur could also stab an attacker with its shoulder spikes.

Spiky defense today

The modern hedgehog can defend itself against attackers by using its spikes, just like *Lexovisaurus* once did.

Size Comparison

A pair of meat-eaters closed in on a *Lexovisaurus*. The plant-eater used its plates and spikes to save itself.

The plates of *Chungkingosaurus* were thick and narrow. They were almost spikes. They may have been used for show. Perhaps *Chungkingosaurus* used its plates to attract other *Chungkingosaurus*. Because it was so spiky, this dinosaur's enemies could have been afraid of it.

Scare tactics today

The modern porcupine fluffs up its quills. Like *Chunkingosaurus'* spikes once did, the porcupine's quills help scare away other animals.

Size Comparison

Chungkingosaurus pawed at the ground and showed its plates to another member of its herd.

HESPEROSAURUS

Hesperosaurus had wide plates along its back. It may have used them to control its body temperature. On a cool day, it might have turned sideways to face the sun. As the plates soaked up the heat, *Hesperosaurus* warmed up. On a hot day, it could have cooled itself by facing the plates into the wind.

Basking today

Modern lizards lie out in the sun to warm themselves up, just like *Hesperosaurus* once did.

Size Comparison

12

In the early morning, *Hesperosaurus* turned its plates to the sun, warming its body.

13

STEGOSAURUS

Pronunciation:
STEG-uh-SAW-rus

Stegosaurus was the biggest of the plated dinosaurs. In addition to the large plates on its back and spikes on its tail, this dinosaur had armored lumps under its neck. The armor protected *Stegosaurus* from meat-eating dinosaurs that went for its throat.

Armored necks today

Like *Stegosaurus* once had, the modern alligator lizard has neck armor, but it is made up of scales.

Size Comparison

Stegosaurus lived on the plains of what is now North America. Armor protected its neck from small meat-eaters.

One of the last of the plated dinosaurs was *Wuerhosaurus*. It was almost as big as *Stegosaurus*. It had long, low plates on its back and sharp spikes on the end of its tail. This dinosaur used the tail spikes to defend itself.

Tail defense today

The modern monitor lizard defends itself with its tail, like *Wuerhosaurus* once did. The lizard uses its tail like a whip.

Size Comparison

Wuerhosaurus swung a spiked tail at a meat-eater to defend itself from attack.

Kentrosaurus lived at the edge of forests. It was a peaceful animal, but the narrow plates and spikes down its back made it look fierce. Meat-eaters stayed away, because they did not want a mouthful of spikes!

Spikes today

The modern horned lizard is covered in spikes, like *Kentrosaurus* once was. The spikes make it look dangerous, even though it is quite harmless.

Size Comparison

18

Kentrosaurus had a small head. It also had a beak that it used to pick leaves and plants.

Yingshanosaurus had two rows of spikey plates along its back. There were also spikes on its tail and shoulders. The shoulder spikes were long and looked like wings. They may have been used as a display to other *Yingshanosaurus* dinosaurs.

Showing off today

The modern cassowary bird has wattles, or showy lumps of skin. As *Yingshanosaurus* once displayed its spikes, the cassowary bird displays its wattles to other birds.

Size Comparison

Yingshanosaurus lived in the forests of what is now China. It moved slowly and quietly between the trees, feeding on plants that covered the ground.

WHERE DID THEY GO?

Dinosaurs are extinct, which means that none of them are alive today. Scientists study rocks and fossils to find clues about what happened to dinosaurs.

People have different explanations about what happened. Some people think a huge asteroid that hit Earth caused all sorts of climate changes, which caused the dinosaurs to die. Others think volcanic eruptions caused the climate change and that killed the dinosaurs. No one knows for sure what happened to all of the dinosaurs.

GLOSSARY

armor—a protective covering of plates, horns, spikes, or clubs used for fighting

beak—the hard front part of the mouth of birds and some dinosaurs; also known as a bill

display—when an animal behaves in a certain way to attract another member of its kind

herd—a large group of animals that moves, feeds, and sleeps together

plates—large, flat, usually tough structures on the body

scutes—pieces of bony armor set into the skin of a dinosaur

spike—a sharp, pointed growth

To Learn More

More Books to Read

Clark, Neil, and William Lindsay. *1001 Facts About Dinosaurs.* New York: Dorling Kindersley, 2002.

Dixon, Dougal. *Dougal Dixon's Amazing Dinosaurs.* Honesdale, Penn.: Boyds Mills Press, 2007.

Holtz, Thomas R., and Michael Brett-Surman. *Jurassic Park Institute Dinosaur Field Guide.* New York: Random House, 2001.

On the Web

FactHound offers a safe, fun way to find Web sites related to topics in this book. All of the sites on FactHound have been researched by our staff.

1. Visit www.facthound.com

2. Type in this special code: 1404840141

3. Click on the FETCH IT button.

Your trusty FactHound will fetch the best Web sites for you!

Index

Look for all of the books in the Dinosaur Find series: